A Companion Anthology to *Literature for Teaching*

Solo Vocal Repertoire for Singers and Teachers of Singers

Tenor Edition

by
Christopher Arneson and Lauren Athey-Janka

Inside View Press

Solo Vocal Repertoire for Singers and Teachers of Singers
Tenor Edition

by

Christopher Arneson
&
Lauren Athey-Janka

ISBN: 978-0-9910876-5-5

Printed in the United States of America

Inside View Press
Gahanna, Ohio
www.VoxPed.com

Introduction

The intent of this book is to provide tools that will help students and teachers achieve their pedagogic goals.
The repertoire we have chosen, along with the technical instructions provided in this book, will guide
the teaching of breathing and breath support, phonation, registration, resonance, and articulation.
Translations and phonetic transcriptions are provided for each selection
to help students explore musical and emotional expression.

For a better understanding of the technical concepts employed in the selection and preparation of the
repertoire that is included in this volume, please refer to:

Literature for Teaching: A Guide for Teaching Solo Vocal Repertoire from a Developmental Perspective
by Christopher Arneson with Lauren Athey-Janka, Inside View Press, 2014

Acknowledgements

The authors extend their sincerest thanks to the following people:

Nicolette Biddle
Josh Bodanza
Alexander Brousseau
Andrew Gavin
Lauren Gilmore
Vicky Nooe
Mike Parisi
Kathryn Pepe
Elisabeth Pirolli
Robert Sickles
Dan Sullivan

Solo Vocal Repertoire for Singers and Teachers of Singers
Tenor Edition

Table of Contents

I.P.A. GUIDE: VOWELS

Forward vowels:	[i]	cheese	*Back vowels:*	[u]	rude
	[I]	hip		[ʊ]	hook
	[e]	hey		[o]	rope
	[ɛ]	wed		[ɔ]	raw
	[æ]	bad		[ɑ]	father
	[a]	mama			

Central vowels:	[ʌ]	up	*Diphthongs:*	[eɪ]	wait
	[ə]	about		[oʊ]	vote
	[ɝ]	heard, American r		[aɪ]	wine
	[ɒ]	dare, British vocalic r		[aʊ]	couch
	[ɚ]	never, American r		[ɔɪ]	joy
				[ju]	huge

Mixed vowels:	[y]	German: *für*	French: lune
	[Y]	German: *Glück*	
	[ø]	German: *schön*	French: deux
	[œ]	German: *könnte*	French: coeur

French Nasals:	[ɛ̃]	[ɛ] plus nasality	French: *bien* [bjɛ̃] English: fount**ain**
	[ɑ̃]	[ɑ] plus nasality	French: *dans* [dɑ̃] English: h**on**k
	[õ]	[o] plus nasality	French: *bon* [bõ] English: **on**ly
	[œ̃]	[œ] plus nasality	French: *humble* [œ̃blə] English: **un**cle

German Diphthongs:	[aɪ]	German: *meine*	English: mine
	[ao]	German: *Augen*	English: couch
	[ɔø]	German: *Freude*	English: joy

Glottal Stop:	[ʔ]	closure of glottis, as in the expression "uh-oh"

I.P.A. GUIDE: CONSONANTS

Stop plosives:	[p]	pal	*Nasals:*	[m]	mind
	[b]	back		[n]	narrow
	[t]	teach		[ŋ]	sing
	[d]	down			
	[k]	kangaroo			
	[g]	get			

Fricatives:	[f]	finger	*Lateral:*	[l]	laugh
	[v]	victory			
	[θ]	thin			
	[ð]	that			
	[s]	self			
	[z]	zebra			
	[ʃ]	ship			
	[ʒ]	azure			
	[h]	him			

Glides:	[r]	rose (American English)	*Combined:*	[tʃ]	chip
	[j]	yellow		[dʒ]	jump
	[ʍ]	what, unvoiced			
	[w]	way, voiced			

Trill, Tap, or flip:	[ɾ]	Italian: *moro* (single flip R)
	[r]	Italian: *ride* (trilled R)
	[r. r]	Italian: *terra* (prolonged trilled R)

Enya: [ɲ]   English: onion   Italian: *regno* [reɲɔ]   French: *vignes* [viɲə]

Elya: [ʎ]   English: million   Italian: *figlio* [fiʎɔ]

French Glide: [ɥ]   French: lui [lɥi] (pronounce [y] then quickly move to [i])

German ichlaut: [ç]   English: hue   German: *dich* [diç]

German achlaut: [χ]   German: *nacht* [naχt]

A Basic Guide to Vocal Exercises
for Beginning Singing Teachers

The questions we are asked most frequently concern the use and function of vocal exercises, or *vocalises*. These inquiries often come from young, aspiring voice teachers and singers, so it seems appropriate to discuss their application.

One of the main reasons for using vocal exercises is to establish good singing technique. But while singing teachers likely agree that voice training must address issues of posture and alignment, respiration, phonation, registration, resonation, and articulation, there is little consensus about the specific types of exercises that should be used. Vocal exercises themselves have no intrinsic value; their effectiveness is measured by how they are applied and under what conditions they are used. Vocal exercises can be designed to help singers achieve optimal onset (initiation of the tone), placement, resonance, breath support, phrasing, legato, staccato, agility, range, vowel clarity, consonants, intonation, and coordination of registers (consecutive pitches with similar timbre that are produced with the same vocal mechanism).

Pre-phonatory exercises involving relaxation, posture, and alignment are essential. Working with students to free specific areas of tension, including muscles of the jaw, tongue, and neck, and helping them to understand the importance of a well-aligned body is the first order of business (e.g. spine elongated, neck back, sternum out, pelvis tucked under, knees unlocked).

The goal of a balanced **ONSET**, or the easy, clean initiation of tone, is usually achieved with simple exercises that feature repeated notes with a breath in between each repetition. Voiced consonants facilitate resonance, tonal efficiency, and clean, clear onsets. An audible, aspirate [h] often is used in staccato or panting exercise, quickly moving on to an inaudible, or imaginary [h].

PLACEMENT refers to the physical sensations experienced while singing. Exercises involving nasal consonants, the vowels [e] and [i], and staccato exercises using voiced consonants, often are used to increase the awareness of resonance sensations in the mask (the general area of the cheekbones).

Maximizing **RESONANCE** is one of the chief goals of classical singing; humming often is used as exercise for this purpose. The colloquial, affirmative "mm-hmm" and the nasal consonant [ng], often also are used to increase sensations of resonance, along with the sibilants [s] and [z] followed by vowels.

The coordination of expiration and phonation, called **BREATH SUPPORT** (breath management), can be developed through the use of pulsation exercises on repeated notes (e.g. [a, a, a, a]), staccato, and the *messa di voce* (crescendo-decrescendo). Lip trills also help to develop breath management skills, as do voiced sibilant and fricative consonants [z] and [v].

LEGATO is consistent phonation, uninterrupted by changing pitches or words, and is one of the most desirable aspects of beautiful singing. Glissandos (slides) can be helpful in introducing the idea of legato, followed by intervallic skip, slurring between each skip. Changing vowels on a slow scale or repeated tones with a single vowel also are useful exercises.

STACCATO is produced much in the same way as legato but without sustaining the sound between each note. Simple scales and repeated notes with a vowel preceded by [h] or [b] and simple arpeggiated chords using "hip" and "yuh" teach staccato effectively. Staccato exercises also help to develop onset and breath coordination.

PHRASING is the grouping of notes into specific units for an artistic or technical purposes. Exercises that develop legato and breath management can help to teach phrasing. Sustained scales, arpeggios and exercises with strategically placed breaths also develop the breath control skills necessary for long phrases.

AGILITY, the execution of fast moving passages with clear articulation, accuracy, and freedom, promotes flexibility and coordination and is of primary importance in good singing. Fast arpeggios and ascending/descending scales using the vowels [u] and [a] (or alternating vowels) help to develop agility.

RANGE extension is accomplished by singing ascending and descending scales and arpeggios, using five, eight, nine, eleven, and sixteen tones. A variety of vowels can be used alone and in combination.

VOWEL clarity, unification, equalization, differentiation, and evenness also must be taught. The production of a free, consistent scale throughout the vocal range with distinct, clear vowels on every pitch is paramount to good singing (voice acoustics makes this nearly impossible for women singing their highest pitches). A neutral tongue position from which all other vowels can be produced will help to develop vowel clarity. Simple arpeggios that alternate front and back vowels such as [a-o-i-o], also are useful.

CONSONANTS, especially voiced consonants, frequently are used in vocal exercises to develop coordinated onset and resonance. Scale patterns, repeated notes, arpeggios, and thirds are useful, with consonants articulated on every note. Initial, medial, and final consonants should be included, and paired unvoiced and voiced consonants are beneficial. Exercises using consonants help to create freedom and flexibility in the articulators (jaw, tongue, and lips).

Exercises for the **COORDINATION of REGISTERS** to promote a seamless, consistent vocal scale usually begin in the area just above or below the register break or *passaggio*. A vocalise consisting of two pitches moving slowly from one to the next and modulating up and down through the *passaggio* is helpful. A variety of vowels may be used on short scales, followed by short arpeggios and interval skips. Closed vowels often are used for men in the upper *passaggio* (above Middle-C, also known as C^4) and for women in the lower *passaggio* (also above Middle-C). Alternating between the vowels [u] and [a] can help singers coordinate the registers.

Descending arpeggios from the head voice in women and falsetto in men, and the use of sirens (vocal slides) also are beneficial.

Ingo Titze, one of our foremost voice scientists, lists "The Five Best Vocal Warmup Exercises" in Volume 57, No.3, 2001 of the *Journal of Singing*:

- Lip trill and tongue trill
- Two octave pitch glides
- Forward tongue roll and extension
- *Messa di voce* (crescendo-decrescendo)
- Staccato on arpeggios

By taking into account the criteria we use to judge whether a tone is functional and/or beautiful—easy onset, legato, clear diction, bright/dark tone quality, excellent breath management skills—we can make decisions as to which exercises might help students best achieve these goals. Keeping a record of what we see and hear in our initial consultation with a singer can serve as a basis for the vocalises that subsequently are developed and utilized.

Students must understand that a secure singing technique can be achieved through regular use of vocal exercises, which should be described in a simple and objective manner. All exercises should be tailored to serve the needs of individual students; few really are needed, provided every aspect of technique is addressed. Many teachers believe that it is essential to assign a specific sequence of vocal exercises, which often follow the major areas of vocal technique, including posture, respiration, phonation, resonance, support, registration, articulation. While this strategy might prove helpful, it is not required.

There are numerous books of vocalises still in print by the 19th century singing masters, including Sieber, Vaccai, Concone and Marchesi. All were well-known teachers and their exercises, along with those of contemporary authors such as William Vennard, Richard Miller, Oren Brown and James McKinney, can help young teachers get started.

A Vocal Exercise Bibliography

Brown, Oren L. (1996). *Discover Your Voice*. San Diego, CA: Singular Publishing Group, Inc.

Coffin, B. (1980). *Overtones of Bel Canto*. Metuchen, NJ: The Scarecrow Press, Inc.

Concone, J. (1898). *Thirty Daily Exercises for the Voice*. New York: G. Schirmer, Inc.

Garcia, M., II. (1975) *A Complete Treatise on the Art of Singing: Part Two* (D. V. Paschke, Ed. and Trans.). New York: Da Capo Press.

Lamperti, G. B. (1905). *The Techniques of Bel Canto* (M. Heidrich. Ed., T. Baker, Trans.). New York: G. Schirmer.

Marchesi, S. (1970) *Bel Canto: A Theoretical and Practical Vocal Method*. London: Enoch and Sons, Ltd., n.d.; reprint, New York: Dover Publications.

McKinney, J. C. (1982) *The Diagnosis and Correction of Vocal Faults*. Nashville, TN: Broadman Press.

Miller, R. (1986). *The Structure of Singing*. New York: Schirmer Books.

Reid, C. L. (1965). *The Free voice: A Guide to Natural Singing*. New York: Coleman-Ross Company, Inc.

Sieber, Ferdinand (1899). *Thirty-Six Eight-Measure Vocalises for Soprano*: op. 92: Volume 111 of Schirmer's library of music classics.

Sieber, Ferdinand (1899). *Thirty-Six Eight-Measure Vocalises for Mezzo-Soprano*: op. 93: Volume 112 of Schirmer's library of music classics.

Sieber, Ferdinand (1899). *Thirty-Six Eight-Measure Vocalises for Alto*: op. 94: Volume 113 of Schirmer's library of music classics.

Sieber, Ferdinand (1899). *Thirty-Six Eight-Measure Vocalises for Tenor*: op. 95: Volume 114 of Schirmer's library of music classics.

Sieber, Ferdinand (1899). *Thirty-Six Eight-Measure Vocalises for Baritone*: op. 96: Volume 115 of Schirmer's library of music classics.

Sieber, Ferdinand (1899). *Thirty-Six Eight-Measure Vocalises for Bass*: op. 97: Volume 116 of Schirmer's library of music classics.

Vennard, W. (1967). *Singing: The Mechanism and the Technic* (rev. ed.). Boston: Carl Fischer, Inc.

Amor mi tiene in pugno

Italian
Stefano Donaudy

Respiration and Support
The quick, syllabic text setting in this piece demands efficient breath support.

Speak the words of the song while pulsing the abdominal muscles and feel an engagement below the sternum with each pulsation, which will engage the body and the muscles of breathing.

Next, sing the melody on [ði] while continuing to pulse the abdominal muscles.

Finally, sing each phrase on [ði]. Rather than pulsing for each word, feel one long in and up movement of the abdominal muscles. Release the abdominal muscles before each phrase, inhale, and repeat.

Resonance
Syllabic texts can make it difficult to achieve consistent resonance. Establishing a vocal roadmap for a singer to rely on is the first step for consistent resonance.

Sing the vocal line on the consonant [m] with the lips together and the teeth apart. The jaw should feel long and the pharynx should feel open. Find resonance within this position, and then place the text within that line of resonance.

Phonation
Ascending and descending phrases are found throughout this piece. To practice vibrant, free phonation, imitate a ghost with spooky and ghost-like [u] that vibrates and moves up and down in pitch.

The vibrancy and freedom found in spooky and ghost-like sounds will influence full-voiced [u].

Start the first note of the scale on ghost-like [u]. During the descent, transition into full-voiced [u].
Maintain vibrancy during the descent.

Registration
Dynamics vary greatly in this piece, ranging from *ppp* (pianississimo) to *mf* (mezzo forte). This dynamic variability provides an excellent opportunity to teach mixed or balanced registration.

The exercise below will introduce the lighter, mixed quality that is needed. Sing [u] in falsetto, change to [y] in *voix mixte*, and then back to [u] in falsetto.

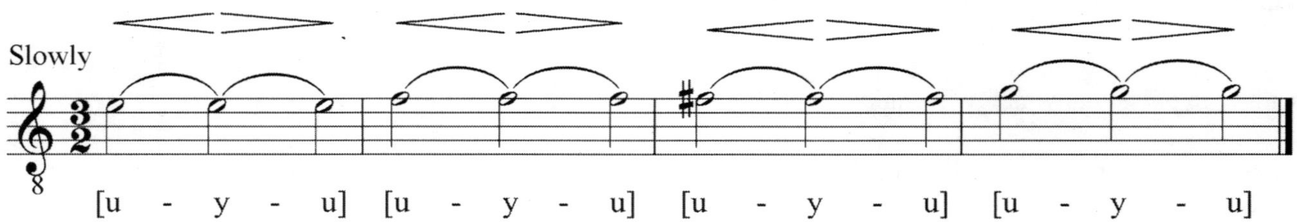

Diction/Articulation
Dialects in Southern Italy, such as Donaudy's home town of Palermo, are quite different from those found inother parts of the country. This song is written in a Southern Neapolitan dialect, where the initial consonant of a word often is doubled when both written and spoken.

Find Southern Italian dialects on YouTube and observe the sounds, mouth positions and syllabic stresses. Many Italian comedians on television shows provide great examples of these sounds. Spend time studying the *dialetti italiani*. This is a fun example:

https://dotsub.com/view/faf04ac9-8a1b-4cbf-9808-e8736ae0fc6e

Next, practicing doubling the initial consonants in these examples. Apply this consonant energy when singing this song.

['puɲ.ɲo] becomes [p.'puɲ.ɲo]
['brut.to] becomes [b.'brut.to]
['reɲ.ɲo] becomes [r.'reɲ.ɲo]
['luŋ:gi] becomes [l.'luŋ:gi]
['tɛn.to] becomes [t.'tɛn.to]

Phonetic Transcription and Translation of the Text

Amor   mi tiene in pugno,
[a.ˈmoːr mi ˈtjɛː.ne in ˈpuɲ.ɲo]
Love holds me tight in its fist,

mi gira   rigira,   m'annusa e poi   sospira…
[mi ˈd͡ʒiː.ɾa ri:ˈd͡ʒiː.ɾa man.ˈnuː.za e poːi so.ˈspiː.ɾa]
it turns me, turns me again, studies me, and then sighs…

Ahimé, che brutto   segno!
[aːi.ˈme ke ˈbrut.to ˈseɲ.ɲo]
Alas, what a nasty sign!

Son già forse indegno   d'entrar nel suo   regno
[soːn d͡ʒa ˈfor.se in:ˈdeɲ.ɲo dɛn.ˈtraːr nel suːo ˈreɲ.ɲo]
Am I perhaps unworthy to enter into his kingdom

e   starvi ancora a   gironzar?
[e ˈstaːr.vi aŋ.ˈkoː.‿ɾa d͡ʒi.ron.ˈdzaːr]
and you remain to stroll about?

Eppur   se adesso   son sì dimesso,
[ep.ˈpuːr se a.ˈdɛs.so so.n si di.ˈmes.so]
And yet if I am now so unworthy,

sparuto,   gibbuto,   sol   buono   a lagrimar,
[spa.ˈɾuː.to d͡ʒib.ˈbuː.to soːl ˈbwɔː.no a la.gri.ˈmaːr]
emaciated, misshapen, only good for weeping,

gli è per quei   sospiri   e i lunghi martiri
[ʎɛ per kweːi so:ˈspiː.ɾi e i ˈluŋːgi mar:ˈtiː.ɾi]
it is through these sighs and long torments

cui   senza ricetto   amor   m'ha costretto…
[kuːi ˈsɛn.tsa ɾi.ˈtʃɛt.to a.ˈmoːr ma ko.ˈstret.to]
that love without hope has forced me…

Ma per un po' ch'io tento qual fui di ritornar,
[ma per un pɔ kiːo ˈtɛn.to kwal fuːi di ɾi.tor.ˈnaːr]
But when I try for a moment to recapture what I was,

vedrete   a cento a cento   le donzellette
[ve.ˈdreː.te a ˈtʃɛn.to a ˈtʃɛn.to le don.dzɛl.ˈlɛt.te]
you will see hundreds of young girls

attorno   a   me   cascar!
[at.ˈtor.no   a   me   ka.ˈskaːr]
falling around me!

D'amor   tal'è   il   costume   davvero   tremendo
[da.ˈmoːr   ta.ˈlɛ   il   ko.ˈstuː.me   dav.ˈveː.ro   tre.ˈmɛn.do]
Such is the truly terrible custom of Love,

che   vivasi   morendo
[ke   vi.ˈvaː.si   mo.ˈrɛn.do]
that one may live dying,

e   che   si   mora   vivi,   di   tutto   già   privi,
[e   ke   si   ˈmɔː.ra   ˈviː.vi   di   ˈtut.to   d͡ʒa   ˈpriː.vi]
and that one may die alive, already deprived of everything,

persin   quando   ancora   molto   c'è   da assaporar…
[pɛr.ˈsiːn   ˈkwan.do   aŋ.ˈkoː.ra   ˈmol.to   t͡ʃɛ   das.sa.po.ˈraːr]
even when there is still much here to savor…

Per   cui   se   adesso   son   sì   dimesso,
[per   kuːi   se   a.ˈdɛs.so   soːn   sì   di.ˈmes.so]
For which if now I am so unworthy,

sparuto,   gibbuto,   sol   buono   a   lagrimar,
[spa.ˈruː.to   d͡ʒib.ˈbuː.to   soːl   ˈbwɔː.no   a   la.gri.ˈmaːr]
emaciated, misshapen, only good for weeping,

gli è   per   quei   sospiri   e i   lunghi   martiri
[ʎɛ   per   kweːi   so.ˈspiː.ri   e i   ˈluŋːgi   mar.ˈtiː.ri]
it is through these sighs and long torments

cui   senza   ricetto   amor   m'ha   costretto…
[kuːi   ˈsɛn.tsa   ri.ˈt͡ʃɛt.to   a.ˈmoːr   ma   ko.ˈstrɛt.to]
that love without hope has forced me…

Ma   per   un po' ch'io   tento   qual   fui   di   ritornar,
[ma   per   un   pɔ   kiːo   ˈtɛn.to   kwal   fuːi   di   ri.tor.ˈnaːr]
But when I try for a moment to recapture what I was,

vedrete   a   cento   a   cento   le   donzellette
[ve.ˈdreː.te   a   ˈt͡ʃɛn.to   a   ˈt͡ʃɛn.to   le   don.dzɛl.ˈlɛt.te]
you will see hundreds of young girls

attorno   a   me   cascar!
[at.ˈtor.no   a   me   ka.ˈskaːr]
falling around me!

Page intentionally left blank to facilitate page turns

Amor mi tiene in pugno

Alberto Donaudy

Stefano Donaudy (1879 - 1925)

p
Meno e rit...
allarg.......
Meno e rit...
mè, che brut-to se - gno! Son già for-se in-de - gno d'en-trar nel suo
a tempo pp leggiero
p dolente cresc.
a tempo
pp
p dolente
cresc.
re-gno e star - vi an - cor-a gi-ron-zar? Ep-pur se a-des - so son si di-mes - so, spa
dim. p dolce
mf a tempo calando e dim.
allarg. u poco rit
allarg. un poco
rit.
a tempo calando e dim.
dim. p mf
ru - to, gib-bu - to, sol buo-no a la-gri-mar gli è per quei so-spi-ri e i

lun - ghi mar - ti - ri cui sen - za ri - cet - to a - mor m'ha co - stret - to. Ma
per un po' ch'io ten - to qual fui di ri - tor - nar, ve - dre-te a cen-to a cen - to le
don - zel - let - te at - tor - no a me ca - scar!

D'a-mor tal'è il co-
stu - me dav - ve - ro tre - men - do che vi-va-si mo-ren-do e che si mo-ra
vi - vi, di tut - to già pri - vi, per - sin quan-do an-co-ra mol - to c'è da as-sa-po-

rar... Per cui se a - des - so son sì di - mes - so, spa - ru - to, gib-
bu - to, sol buo-no a la - gri - mar, gli è per quei so - spi - ri e i lun-ghi mar-
ti - ri cui sen - za ri - cet - to a - mor m'ha co - stret - to Ma per un po' ch'io

dim.
ppp
dolciss.
p
pp
allarg. un poco
79
80 allarg........ 81
82 Meno e rall
83
84
a tempo
ten - to qual fui di ri-tor-nar, ve-dre-te a cen-to a cen-to le don-zel-let-te at
allarg................
Meno e rall.
a tempo
allarg. un poco
dim.
ppp
p
pp
a tempo
ten.
85
86
87
88
89
tor-no a me ca-scar!
col canto
a tempo
f gaio
mf
f
mf
90
91
92
93
94
Meno e rit.
mp
p
pp
11

Cangia, cangia tue voglie

Italian
Giovanni Battista Fasolo

Respiration and Support
In order to prepare for the numerous catch breaths in this piece, inhale quickly and lightly through a straw, noticing that even though the breath is quick, it goes deep into the body.

Resonance
The consonant [k] lifts the soft palate and releases the larynx. Using [k] to balance resonance, as in *cangia, cor, che,* and *crudele*, allow the [k] to spring the sensations above the palate.

Phonation

To teach agility, sing measures 51-55 on [v], and then transition to [v] with the corresponding vowels.

Registration

Isolate the octave interval found in measure 34 using the vowel pattern [o] to [ɔ] to [o]. Maintain the [ɔ] position when singing the word *lascia* on G^4.

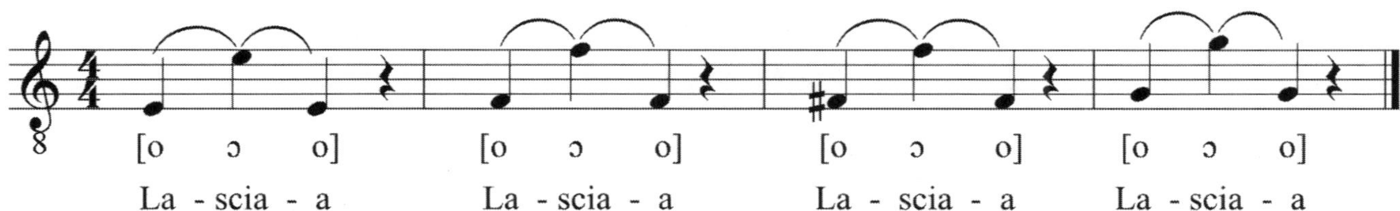

Diction/Articulation

Practice speaking the text from measures 30-40 in rhythm, using the tongue and lips to articulate the text. Be sure that jaw movement is minimal. Next, sing this in rhythm on one pitch using the same articulation.

Non t'accorgi, meschin, che sei ferito?
Lascia, lascia d'amar chi t'ha tradito.
Lascia, lascia d'amar chi t'ha tradito.

Finally, sing this in rhythm on one pitch using the same articulation while keeping a spacious feeling in the mouth.

Phonetic Transcription and Translation of the Text

Cangia,   cangia   tue   voglie, o mio   cor,
[ˈkan.d͡ʒa ˈkan.d͡ʒa tuːe ˈvɔʎ:ʎe o miːo kɔːr]
Change, change your desires, oh my heart,

che   fedele   fosti a   donna   crudele.
[ke fe.ˈdeː.le ˈfo.sti a ˈdɔn.na kru.ˈdɛː.le]
which was faithful to a cruel woman.

Non   t'accorgi   meschin, che sei   ferito?
[non tak.ˈkɔr.d͡ʒi me.ˈskiːn ke sɛːi fe.ˈriː.to]
Don't you realize, wretched one, that you are wounded?

Lascia,   lascia   d'amar   chi t'ha tradito.
[ˈlaʃ.ʃa ˈlaʃ.ʃa da.ˈmaːr ki ta tra.ˈdi.to]
Cease, cease to love the one who has deceived you.

Lascia, lascia   d'amar   chi ti   finge   col   riso,
[ˈlaʃ.ʃa ˈlaʃ.ʃa da.ˈmaːr.r ki ti ˈfin.d͡ʒe kol ˈriː.zo]
Cease, cease to love the one who deceives you with a smile,

col   mostrarti   il   bel   viso.
[kol mo.ˈstraːr.ti il bɛl ˈviː.zo]
showing you her beautiful face.

Vedi   pur   come   il   canto è cagion   di   tue   doglie!
[ˈveː.di puːr ˈkoː.me il ˈkan.to ɛ ka.ˈd͡ʒoːn di tuːe ˈdɔʎ.ʎe]
See indeed how the song is the cause of your suffering!

Cangia,   cangia   tue   voglie.
[ˈkan.d͡ʒa ˈkan.d͡ʒa tuːe ˈvɔʎ:ʎe]
Change, change your wishes.

Non   t'accorgi   meschin, che sei   ferito?
[non tak.ˈkɔr.d͡ʒi me.ˈskiːn ke sɛːi fe.ˈriː.to]
Don't you realize, wretched one, that you are wounded?

Lascia, lascia   d'amar   chi t'ha tradito.
[ˈlaʃ.ʃa ˈlaʃ.ʃa da.ˈmaːr ki ta tra.ˈdi.to]
Cease, cease to love the one who has deceived you.

Cangia, cangia tue voglie

from *Misticanza di vigna alla bergamasca*

cor, che fe-de-le fo-sti a don-na, fo-sti a don-na, fo-sti a don-na cru-de-le.
Non t'ac-cor-gi, me-schin, che sei fe-ri-to? La-scia, la-scia d'a-
mar chi t'ha tra-di-to.... La-scia, la-scia d'a-mar chi t'ha tra-di-to.
cresc.
p
f
p
f
ten.
p
a tempo
dim......... e........ rit...................
a tempo
rit...........
a tempo
rit.
p
dim.
a tempo
mf

La - scia, la - scia d'a - ma - re_ chi_ ti fin - ge col ri - so, col mo - strar - ti il bel
vi - so, col mo - strar - ti il_ bel vi - so. La - scia, la - scia d'a - ma - re_ chi_ ti

fin - ge col ri - so, col mo - strar - ti il bel vi - so, col mo - strar - ti il bel
vi - so. Non t'ac - cor - gi, me - schin, che sei fe - ri -
to? La - scia, la - scia d'a - mar chi t'ha tra - di - to.... La - scia,

80 81 82 rit. 83 84 85 86
la - scia d'a- mar chi t'ha tra-di - to.
rit.
a tempo
rit.

Die Sonne scheint nicht mehr
German
Johannes Brahms

Respiration and Support

A catch breath is needed several times this song. To achieve a low and quick breath, practice panting at a very slow tempo; double the tempo, and finally, double it once more. Be sure that the abdominal muscles release and the lower back expands during the inhalation, and the abdominal muscles move inward and upward during exhalation.

Resonance

With a dramatic tempo marking and emotional transitions, a singer has the opportunity to show many vocal colors in this song. Ask questions regarding these colors. Which might represent sadness? Which represents hope? Which could represent torture? Once a color palette has been determined, mark those colors in the score.

Phonation

The middle section is marked *lebhaft*, which is an indication for a quick and lively tempo.

> Sing this fast melody on [z].
> Sing each note on [zu] in the quick tempo.
> Then sing each phrase on [zu], placing [z] before the first note of the phrase only.
> Visualize the energy gained from [z] when transitioning to text.

In the exercise below, practice building agility by intoning the rhythm of this section on [z]. Next, repeat with the indicated phonemes and text.

Registration

The middle section is faster, which allows the singer to quickly sing through the *passaggio*.

Diction/Articulation

Imagine physically holding a cello while moving the bow through the slurred notes. Feel the legato motion in your arm. Visualize this through the fast, slurred notes to prevent heavy re-articulation.

Notice that many German words end with a *schwa* sound: [ə]. This is a unique speech sound in German that requires practice. Many American singers incorrectly use the wrong sounds. This was Lindsey Christiansen's[1] explanation of *Schwa*:

> After bright vowels, shaded toward [ɛ]: *liebe, schwebe*
> After rounded vowels, shaded toward rounded [ə]: *möchte, rufe*
> When these sounds appear at the end of a word: en, el, es, et, er, shaded toward darker [ə]: *Himmel, Mutter*

Phonetic Transcription and Translation of the Text

Die Sonne scheint nicht mehr
[di: ˈzɔ.nə ˈʃa:ent   nɪçt me:ɐ̯]
The sun no longer shines

So schön, als wie vorher,
[zo: ʃø:n   ʔals vi: fo:ɐ̯ˈhe:ɐ̯]
as beautifully as it did before,

Der Tag ist nicht so heiter,
[de:ɐ̯ ta:k ʔɪst nɪçt zo: ˈha:etɐ]
the day is not as cheerful,

So liebreich gar nicht mehr.
[zo: li:p.raɪç ga:ɐ̯ nɪçt me:ɐ̯]
not as affectionate any more.

Das Feuer kann man löschen,
[das ˈfɔ:ʏ.ɐ kan man lœ.ʃen]
The flame can be extinguished,

Die Liebe nicht vergessen,
[di: ˈli:.bə nɪçt fɛɐ̯.ˈgɛ.sən]
but love cannot be squelched,

Das Feuer brennt so sehr,
[das ˈfɔ:ʏ.ɐ brɛnt   zo: ze:ɐ̯]
the flame does burn brightly,

Die Liebe noch viel mehr.
[di: ˈli:.bə nɔχ fi:l me:ɐ̯]
but love burns stronger still.

Mein Herz ist nicht mehr mein,
[ma:en hɛrts ʔɪst nɪçt me:ɐ̯ ma:en]
My heart is no longer mine.

O könnt ich bei dir sein,
[ʔo: kœnt ʔɪç ba:e di: ɐ̯ za:en]
Oh, may I be near you,

So wäre mir geholfen
[zo: ˈvɛ:.rə mi:ɐ̯ gə.ˈhɔl.fən]
so I could find refuge

Von aller meiner Pein.
[fɔn ˈʔa.lɐ ma:e.nɐ pa:en]
from all my pain

---

[1] Professor Christiansen was a prominent singing teacher who spent most of her career teaching at Westminster Choir College

Die Sonne scheint nicht mehr

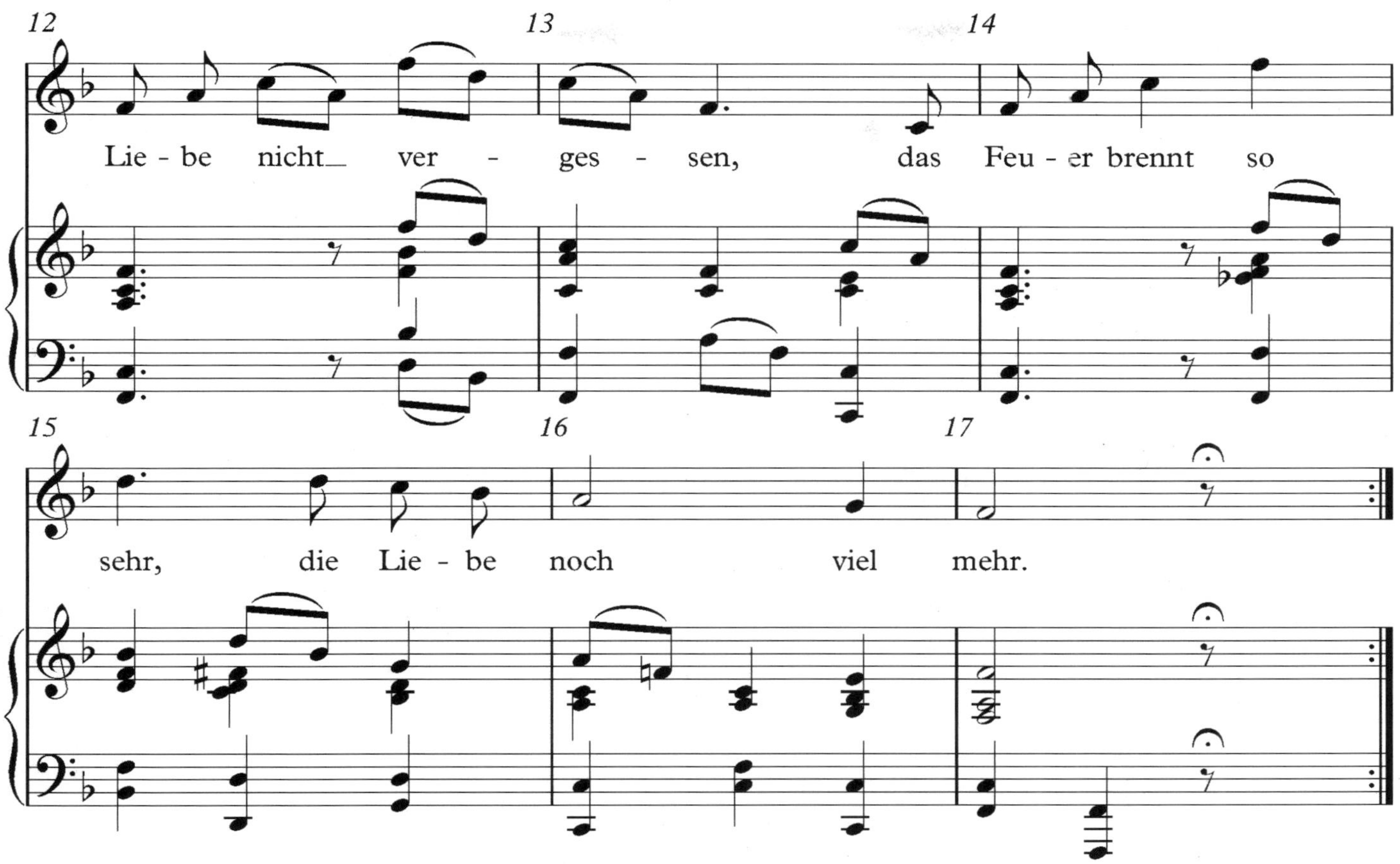

Lie - be nicht__ ver - ges - sen, das Feu - er brennt so
sehr, die Lie - be noch viel mehr.

Stille Sicherheit

German
Robert Franz

Respiration and Support
Practice breathing slowly through the nose, expanding the lower back first, followed by the ribcage. The inhalation should never cause the muscles of breathing to lock. Exhale slowly, through pursed lips, feeling the lower abdominal muscles gently pull in as breath is released.

Resonance
To ensure the voice is even throughout its range and that resonance is consistent over changing pitch, sing this vocalise on one vowel. Be sure that the vowel is clear. Repeat this exercise in various keys.

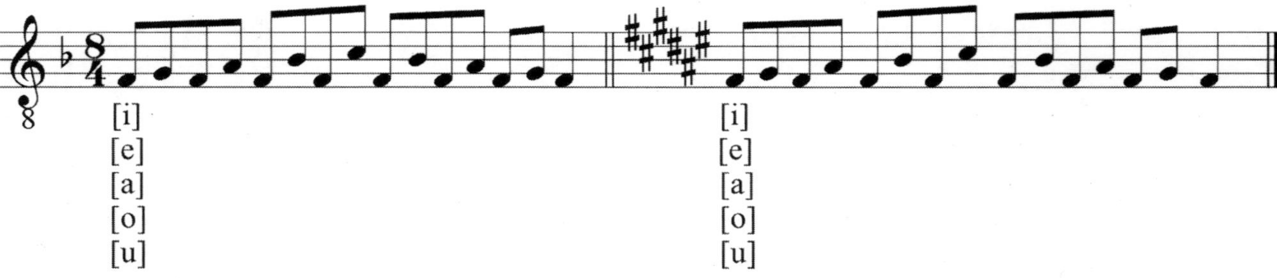

Phonation
First, practice *messa di voce* (*crescendo/decrescendo* without taking a breath) on a lip trill and [v] on various pitches to practice the dynamic changes in this song.

Next, practice the following exercise using the dynamics that are marked and in varioius keys.

Registration

Sing this vocalise with the following vowel sequence (closed to open) to align registration:

Diction/Articulation

These exercises will develop the specific sounds of the German language, such as "*Ich-Laut*" [ç] and "*Ach-Laut*" [χ].

The sound in *Ich-Laut* [ç] can be found in the American English:

Houston
Huge
Humid
Human
Hugh

The *Ach-Laut* [χ] is caused by friction in the air as it passes through the throat, and may include a uvular rattle. Speak the name Bach, and feel the friction behind the tongue.

Phonetic Transcription and Translation of the Text

Horch, wie still es wird im dunklen Hain,
[hɔrç viː ʃtɪl ʔɛs vɪrt ʔɪm ˈdʊŋk.lən haːen]
Listen, how quiet it becomes in the dark grove,

Mädchen, wir sind sicher und allein.
[ˈmɛːt.çən viː ɐ̯ zɪnt ˈzɪ.çɒ ʔʊnt ʔa.ˈlaːen]
maiden, we are safe and alone.

Still versäuselt (umsäuselt) hier am Wiesenhang
[ʃtɪl fɛɐ̯.ˈzɔːʏ.zəlt (ʔʊm.ˈzɔːʏ.zəlt) hiːɐ̯ ʔam ˈviː.zən.ˌha]
Quietly murmurs (murmurs) here on the meadow slope

Schon der Abendglocken müder Klang.
[ʃoːn deːɐ̯ ˈʔaː.bənt.ˌglɔ.kən ˈmyː.dɐ klaŋ]
already the evening bell's tired sound.

Auf den Blumen, die sich dir verneigt,
[ʔaːof deːn ˈbluː.mən diː zɪç diːɐ̯ fɛɐ̯.ˈnaːekt]
On the flowers, which have bowed themselves to you,

Schlief das letzte Lüftchen ein und schweigt.
[ʃliːf das ˈlɛts.tə ˈlʏft.çən ʔaːen ʔʊnt ʃvaːekt]
the last breeze falls asleep and is silent.

Sagen darf ich dir, wir sind allein,
[ˈzaː.gən darf ʔɪç diːɐ̯ viːɐ̯ zɪnt ʔa.ˈlaːen]
I may tell you, for we are alone,

Dass mein Herz ist ewig ewig dein.
[das maːen hɛrts ʔɪst ˈʔeː.vɪç ˈʔeː.vɪç daːen]
that my heart is eternally, eternally yours.

Stille Sicherheit

Op. 10 N. 2

Nikolaus Lenau

Robert Franz
(1815-1892)

A - bend - glo - cken mü - der Klang.
Auf den Blu - men, die sich dir ver-neigt, schlief das
letz - te Lüft-chen ein und schweigt. Sa-gen darf ich dir,

pp
mf
cresc.
wir sind al - lein,
das mein Herz ist
cresc.
mf
cresc.
f
e - wig, e - wig Dein.
f
dim.
p

Le Soir

French
Charles Gounod

Respiration and Support

The accompaniment provides a steady pulse, which helps to maintain flexible and buoyant breath support. Sing the melody on the subdivided rhythms sown below:

Resonance

The French language is a brighter sounding than American English. To help maintain this quality, speak the French nasal vowels, moving from nasal- to non-nasal resonance. Alternate each vowel with its nasal counter-part.

1. [ɛ] to [ɛ̃] to [ɛ]
2. [ɑ] to [ɑ̃] to [ɑ]
3. [o] to [õ] to [o]
4. [œ] to [œ̃] to [œ]

Phonation

This text contains many voiced and voiceless fricatives, including [s], [z] and [ʃ]. Hold a hand in front of the mouth while singing to feel the continuous stream of air through the speech sounds that help to create a vibrant tone.

Registration

Using [œ], [y] and [ɛ̃], which appear frequently on the highest pitches in this piece, sing an ascending arpeggio on these vowels.

Diction/Articulation

Practice speaking the text with no syllabic stress, aiming for an even and continuous lyric line.

Next, practice chanting the melody.

Phonetic Transcription and Translation of the Text

Le soir ramène le silence.
[lə swaɾ ɾa.mɛ.nə lə si.lɑ̃.sə]
The evening brings back the silence.

Assis sur ces rochers déserts,
[a.si syɾ sɛ ɾɔ.ʃe de.zɛɾ]
Seated upon these rocks deserted,

Je suis dans le vague des airs
[ʒe sɥi dɑ̃ lə va.gə dɛ.‿zɛɾ]
I contemplate

Le char de la nuit qui s'avance.
[lə ʃaɾ də la nɥi ki sa.vɑ̃.s.v
the chariot of the night approaches.

Vénus se lève à l'horizon;
[ve.ny sə lɛ.‿va lɔ.ɾi.zõ]
Venus itself rises on the horizon;

À mes pieds l'étoile amoureuse
[a me pje le.twa.‿la.mu.ɾø.zə]
at my feet the star of love

De sa lueur mystérieuse
[də sa ly.œɾ mi.ste.ɾi.ø.zə]
with its mysterious glow

Blanchit les tapis de gazon.
[blɑ̃.ʃi lgazon.e gazon. gazo
whitens the carpet of the grass.

Tout à coup détaché de cieux,
[tu.‿ta ku de.ta.ʃe də sjø]
All of a sudden from the heavens detaches

Un rayon de l'astre nocturne,
[œ ɾɛ.jõ də las.tɾə nɔk.tyɾ:nə]
a ray of light from the evening star,

Glissant sur mon front taciturne,
[glis.sɑ̃ sỹne,sur mon front ng star,,he
falling upon my silent brow,

Vient mollement toucher mes yeux.
[vjɛ̃ mɔ.lə.mɑ̃ tu. mɔ.eux. toucher
comes to touch my eyes gently

Doux reflet d'une globe de flamme,
[du rə.flɛ dy.nə glɔ.bə də flɑ.mə]
Gentle reflection of a fiery orb,

Charmant rayon que me veux- tu?
[ʃaɾ.mɑ̃ tu?ux- tu?ue me veux- tu? fla
charming light, what do you wish of me?

Viens- tu dans mon sein abattu
[vjɛ̃ ty dɑ̃ mõ sɛ̃.‿na.ba.ty]
Have you come to my weary breast

Porter la lumière à mon âme?
[pɔɾ.te la ly.mjɛ.‿ɾa mõ.‿nɑ:mə]
to bring the light to my soul?

Descends- tu pour me révéler
[də.sɑ̃ ty puler me révélerâme
Have you come down in order to reveal to me

Des mondes le divin mystère?
[de mõ.də lə di.vɛ̃ mis.tɛ.ɾə]
the divine mystery of the world?

Ces secrets cachés dans la sphère
[sɛ sə.krɛ ka.ʃe dɑ̃ la sfɛ.rə]
Those secrets hidden in the sphere

Où le jour va te rappeler?
[u lə ʒur va tə ra.pə.le]
to where daylight will summon you?

Viens- tu dévoiler l'avenir
[vjɛ̃ ty de.vwa.le la.və.niɾ]
Have you come to unveil the future

Au cœur fatigué qui t'implore?
[o kœɾ fa.ti.ge ki tɛ̃.plɔ.rə]
to a weary heart that implores you?

Rayon divin, es- tu l'aurore
[rɛ.jõ di.vɛ̃ ɛ ty lo.rɔ.rə]
Ray divine, are you the dawn

Du jour qui ne doit pas finir?
[dy ʒur ki nə dwa pɑ fi.niɾ]
of the day that will never end?

Page intentionally left blank to facilitate page turns

Le Soir

à Mme. Pauline Viardot

A. de Lamartine

Charles Gounod
(1818-1893)

serts_____ Je suis dans le va - gue des airs le char de la nuit qui s'a van -
p   pp

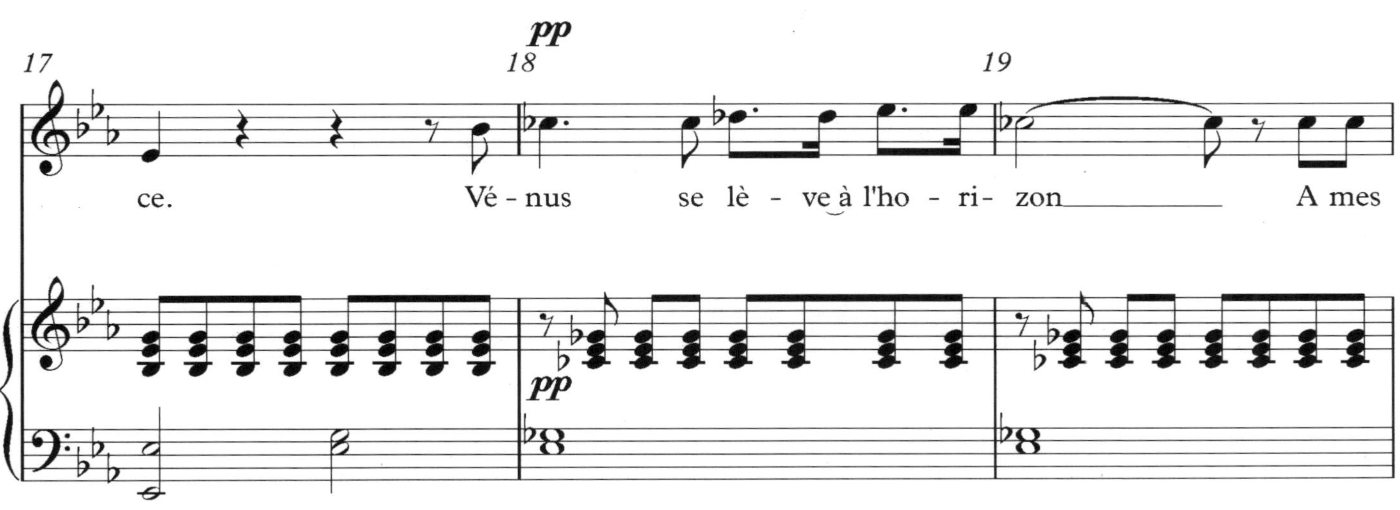

pp
ce. Vé - nus se lè - ve à l'ho - ri - zon_____ A mes
pp

pieds l'é toi - le a - mou - reu - se De sa lu - eur my - sté - ri -

23
24
25
26
eu - se Blan-chit les ta-pis de ga-zon____ Tout à coup dé-ta-ché des
p

27
28
cresc.
29
cieux____ Un ra-yon de l'as-tre noc-tur - ne, Glis-
cresc - - - - scen - - - - - do

30
31
32
sant sur mon front ta-ci-tur - ne, Vient mol-le-ment,____ vient mol-le-
f
dim.
p

33
ment tou-cher mes yeux!
pp
34
35
p
36
37
38
39
40
cresc - - - - scen - - - - - do - -
41
42
43
44
Doux re-flet d'un glo-be de
dim.
p
pp

45
46
47
flam - me, Char - mant ra - yon, que me veux - tu?________ Viens -

48
49
50
tu dans mon sein a-bat-tu por-ter la lu - miè - re à mon â -
p
pp

51
52
53
me De - scends - tu pour me ré - vé - ler Des
pp

mon - des le di - vin my - stè - re Ces se -crets ca - chés dans la

sphè - re Où le jour va le rap -pe - ler?__________ Viens -

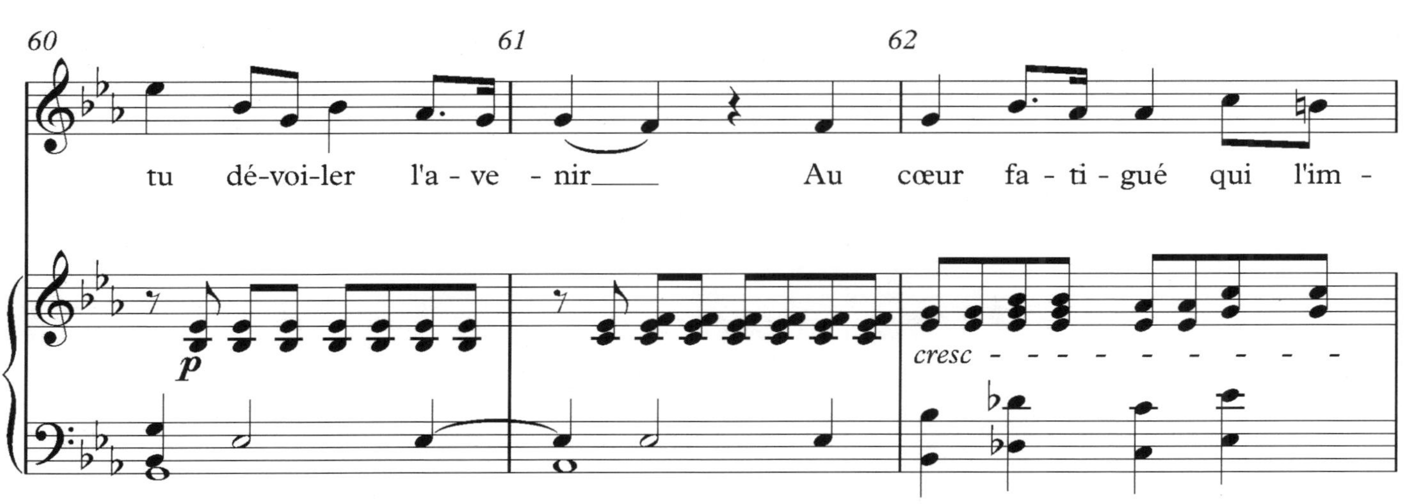

tu dé -voi-ler l'a - ve - nir_____ Au cœur fa - ti - gué qui l'im -
cresc - - - - - - - - -
p

63
64
65
plo - re Ra - yon,_______ ra - yon di - vin,____ es - tu l'au -
f
dim.
p

66
67
68
ro - re Du jour__________ qui ne doit pas fi - nir?
pp

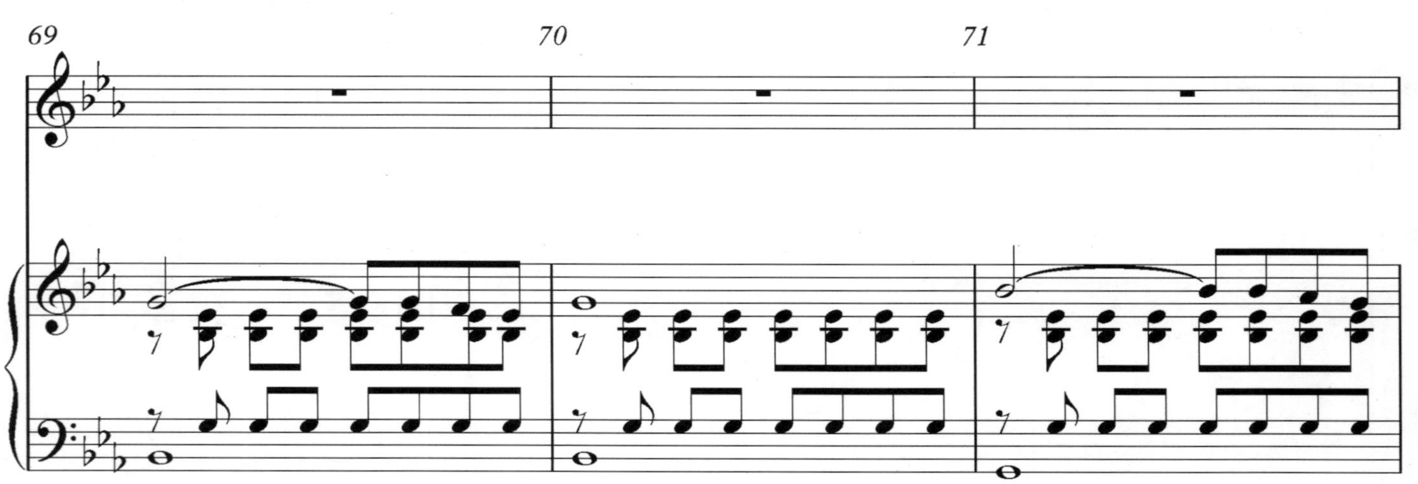
69
70
71

72
73
74
cresc - - - - scen - - - - - do - -
75
76
77
dim.
rit. - - - - - -
78
79
80
pp
41

Élégie

French
Jules Massenet

Respiration and Support

Dotted rhythms, which appear in many phrases of this song, help singers avoid tension in the muscles of breathing. Practice this vocalise in various keys and vowels to instill these habits.

Resonance

The quality of French vowels can help to build consistent resonance in young singers. To develop an awareness of the unique resonance quality in the French language, which is very different from American English, intone the vowels in measures 21 and 22.

Comme en mon coeur tout est sombre et glacé!

[kɔ. mã mɔ̃ kœr tu. tɛ sɔ̃. bʀe gla.se]

[ɔ ã ɔ̃ œ u ɛ ɔ̃ e a e]

Phonation

Frequent shifts in dynamics are seen throughout this song. Sing a lip trill on various pitches practice moving from *pp* to *mf* to *ff* to *mf* to *pp* to balance breath pressure and vocal fold vibration. This is the first step for training *messa di voce*.

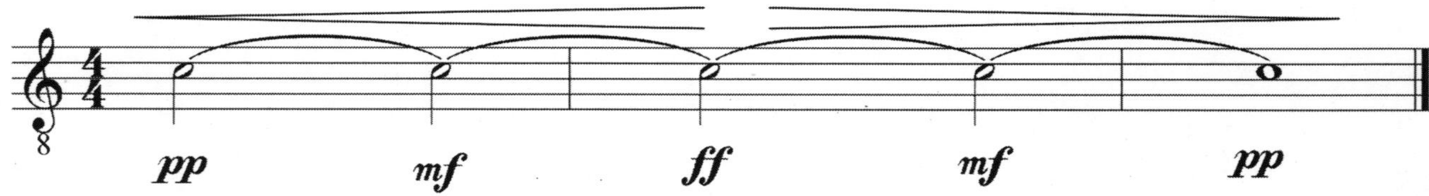

Registration

This song teaches the singer to maintain a stable laryngeal position in descending passages because of the various closed vowels in the French language. Sing measures 3-8 (below) without consonants, and then repeat with the complete text.

Diction/Articulation

The French language includes the closed [o], which requires rounded lips. Using a mirror, practice moving from an American [o] without rounded lips to a French [o] with rounded and protruded lips. This position must be carried into the rounded and mixed vowels that appear.

Phonetic Transcription and Translation of the Text

Ô, doux printemps d'autre fois, vertes saisons,
[o du   prɛ̃.tɛ̃   do.trə   fwa   vɛˌrtə   sɛˌzɔ̃]
Oh, sweet spring of another time, seasons of green,

Vous avez fui pour toujours!
[vu‿za,vɛ   fɥi   pur   tuˌʒurˌ]
you have fled forever!

Je ne vois plus le ciel bleu;
[ʒə   nə   vwa   ply   lə   sjəl   blø]
I can no longer see the blue sky;

Je n'entends plus les chants joyeux des oiseaux!
[ʒə   nɑ̃ˌt   nɑ̃entends   plus   les   chants   joyeux   des   oiseaux!meri
I no longer hear the joyous songs of the birds!

En emportant mon bonheur, mon bonheur...
[ɑ̃‿nɑ̃,pɔr.tɑ̃   mɔ̃   bɔ.nør   mɔ̃   bɔ.nør]
And taking away my happiness, my happiness...

Ô bien-aimé, tu t'en es allé!
[o   bjɛ̃‿nɛ.me   tɥ   tɑ̃‿nɛ‿za.le]
Oh, beloved, you have gone away!

Et   c'est en   vain   que   revient   le   printemps!
[e   sɛ.t̪ã   vɛ̃   kə   rə.vjɛ̃   lə   prɛ̃.t̪ã]
And it is in vain that the spring returns!

Oui,   sans   retour,
[ɥi   sã   rə.tuɾ]
Yes, never to return,

avec   toi,   le   gai   soleil,
[a.vɛk   twa   lə   gɛ   sɔ.lɛj]
with you gone, the sun shines no more,

Les   jours riants   sont   partis!
[le   ʒu.‿ɾjã   sɔ̃   paɾ.ti]
the smiling days have disappeared!

Comme en   mon   coeur   tout est   sombre et   glacé!
[kɔ.m̪ã   mɔ̃   kœr   tu.t̪ɛ   sɔ̃.‿brе   gla.se]
Like my heart, all is dark and cold!

Tout est   flétri
[tu.‿t̪ɛ   fle.tɾi]
All is withering

pour toujours!
[puɾ   tu.ʒuɾ]
for always!

Élégie

Jules Massenet
(1842-1921)
Triste et très lent
p trés expressif avec accablement
Ô___ doux prin - temps d'au-tre-fois,
f
rit.
pp
mf expressif et soutenu
Ped.
mf
Ver - tes sai-sons,
p
Vous a-vez fui pour tou - jours! Je ne vois
mf
espress. imitez le chant
pp
f
plus le ciel bleu;
mf
Je n'en-tends plus
p
les chants joy-eux des oi -

seaux! En em-por-tant mon bon - heur,___ Ô bien-ai- mé, tu t'en es___ allé! Et c'est en vain que re-vient le prin - temps! Oui, sans re -
tour, a-vec toi le gai so- leil, Les jours ri-ants sont par - tis! Comme en mon

22
mf dim. p
23
coeur tout est som - bre et gla - cé! Tout est flé -

pp a tempo
Allargando
p
24 25 26 27
tri! Pour tou jours!
Allargando
pp cresc.
cresc.
ff
8vb
Ped. *

Is my team ploughing?

English
George Butterworth

Butterworth is a British composer, and several of the words in this text might be unfamiliar to Americans. Here are a few examples:

"Team" refers to the horses or oxen that would pull a plow.
"Ploughing" means to turn up soil for cultivation (plowing).
"Chase the leather" refers to running after a ball.
"Thin and pine" refers to his withering body within a pine coffin.
"Cheer" refers to comfort.

Respiration and Support

To prepare for the various lengths of time provided for taking breaths, practice the following exercises:

- Inhale for 4 counts, and then sing the vocal line. Repeat this before every phrase.
- Inhale for 3 counts, and then sing the vocal line. Repeat this before every phrase.
- Inhale for 2 counts, and then sing the vocal line. Repeat this before every phrase.
- Inhale for 1 count, and then sing the vocal line. Repeat this before every phrase.

And then, mark with a colored pencil exactly how many counts are given to breathe before each phrase.

Resonance

Intone the vowels of the text, feeling the sensations of resonance in vowel-to-vowel singing. Be sure to give a greater length of time and attention to the first vowel of each diphthong.

Is my   team ploughing,
[ɪ aːɪ   i   aaaːʊ.i]

That I   was used to drive
[æ aaaːɪ   ɑ   u   u aaaːɪ]

First, sing only with vowels, striving to maintain consistent resonance. Relaxed articulation will encourage consistent resonance when adding the text.

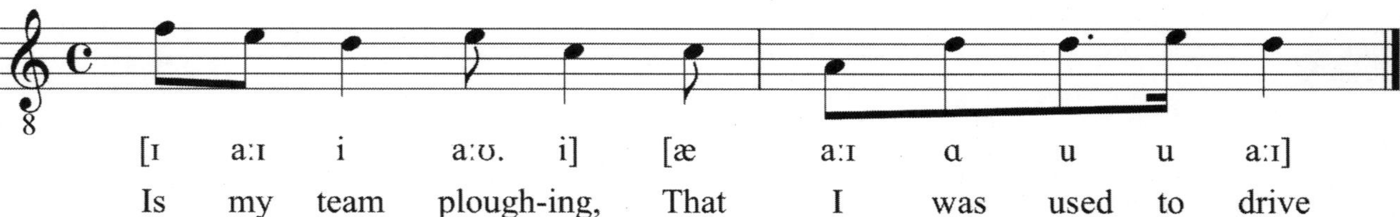

Phonation

A clean onset (not breathy or hard) in mixed voiced (*voix mixte*), may be difficult for a young tenor. Before singing the descending phrase, practice the phrase on [m]. The lips are together, the teeth are apart, and the jaw should feel long. Practice the exercise below before each verses.

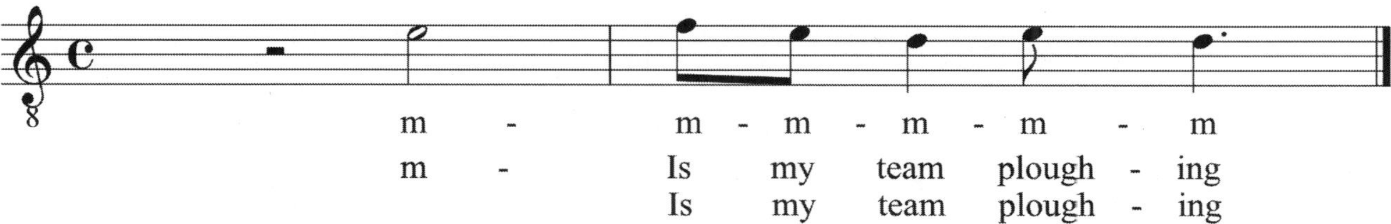

Registration

This piece presents an opportunity to teach *voix mixte*, because the *pianissimo* sections start with descending lines. To find this quality easily, make siren or ghost-like sounds on [u], and then transition to vocalises. Use the exercise below to train head voice.

Diction/Articulation

Intone the text with a British- received accent. Take time to notice the following sounds unique to the language, such as:

Harness
ˈhɑɹ̯.nɪ(ɑɹ̯

horses
ˈhɔɹ̯s.ɪz

trample
ˈtɹæm.pəl

under
ˈʌn.dɐ

river-shore
ˈɹɪ.vɐ.ˈʃɔɹ̯

Phonetic Transcription of the Text

"Is my team ploughing,
[ɪz maːɪ tim 'plaːʊ.ɪŋ]

That I was used to drive
[ðæt aːɪ wɑz just tu dɹaːɪv]

And hear the harness jingle
[ænd hɪɐ̯ ðʌ 'haɐ̯.nəs 'd͡ʒɪŋ.gəl]

When I was man alive?"
[ʍɛn aːɪ wɑz mæn ə.'laːɪv]

Ay, the horses trample,
[aːɪ ðʌ 'hɔɐ̯.səz 'tɹæm.pəl]

The harness jingles now;
[ðʌ 'haɐ̯.nəs 'd͡ʒɪŋ.gəlz naːʊ]

No change though you lie under
[noːʊ t͡ʃeːɪnd͡ʒ ðoːʊ ju laːɪ 'ʌn.dɐ̯]

The land you used to plough.
[ðʌ lænd ju just tu plaːʊ]

"Is football playing
[ɪz 'fʊt.bɔl 'pleːɪ.ɪŋ]

Along the river-shore,
[ə.'lɑŋ ðʌ 'ɹɪ.vɐ̯.ʃɔɐ̯]

With lads to chase the leather,
[wɪð lædz tu t͡ʃeːɪs ðʌ 'lɛ.ðɐ̯]

Now I stand up no more?"
[naːʊ aːɪ stænd ʌp noːʊ mɔɐ̯]

Ay, the ball is flying,
[aːɪ ðʌ bɔl ɪz 'flaːɪ.ɪŋ]

The lads play heart and soul;
[ðʌ lædz pleːɪ haɐ̯t ænd soːʊl]

The goal stands up, the keeper
[ðʌ goːʊl stændz ʌp ðʌ 'ki.pɐ̯]

Stands up to keep the goal.
[stændz ʌp tu 'ki.p ðʌ goːʊl]

"Is my girl happy,
[ɪz maːɪ gɜl 'hæp.i]

that I thought hard to leave,
[ðæt aːɪ θɔt hɑɐ̯d tu liv]

And has she tired of weeping
[ænd hæz ʃi taːɪɐ̯d ɑv 'wip.ɪŋ]

As she lies down at eve?"
[æz ʃi laːɪz daːʊn æt iv]

Ay, she lies down lightly,
[aːɪ ʃi laːɪz daːʊn 'laːɪt.li]

She lies not down to weep:
[ʃi laːɪz nɑt daːʊn tu wip]

Your girl is well contented.
[jɔɐ̯ gɜl ɪz wɛl kən.'tɛn.təd]

Be still, my lad, and sleep.
[bi stɪl maːɪ læd ænd slip]

"Is my friend hearty,
[ɪz maːɪ fɹɛnd 'haɐ̯.ti]

Now I am thin and pine,
[naːʊ aːɪ æm θɪn ænd paːɪn]

And has he found to sleep in
[ænd hæz hi faːʊnd tu slip ɪn]

A better bed than mine?"
[ʌ 'bɛ.tɐ̯ bɛd ðæn maːɪn]

Yes, lad, I lie easy,
[jɛs læd aːɪ laːɪ 'i.zi]

I lie as lads would choose;
[aːɪ laːɪ æz lædz wʊd t͡ʃuz]

I cheer a dead man's sweetheart,
[aːɪ t͡ʃɪɐ̯ ʌ dɛd mænz 'swit.haɐ̯t]

Never ask me whose.
[nɛ.vɐ̯ æsk mi huz]

Page intentionally left blank to facilitate page turns

Is my team ploughing?

10 11 12
long the ri - ver shore, With lads to chase the lea-ther, Now I stand up no more?"
ppp
13 Poco piu mosso 14 15
f
Ay, the ball is fly ing, The lads play heart and soul; The goal stands up, the keep - er Stands
Poco piu mosso
f
16 rit. e dim. Tempo I 17 pp 18 19
up to keep the goal. 'Is my girl hap-py, that I thought hard to leave, And
Tempo I
p colla voce
pp

Poco piu mosso
f
20
21
22
has she tired of weep-ing As she lies down at eve?" Ay, she lies down light-ly, She
Poco piu mosso
ppp
f

Tempo I
23
24
25 rit. e dim.
26
lies not down to weep: Your girl is well con-tent-ed. Be still, my lad, and sleep.
Tempo I
p colla voce
pp

27
pp
28
29
"Is my friend hear-ty, Now I am thin and pine, And has he found to sleep in A

Poco piu mosso
f
Poco piu mosso
ppp
f
bet-ter bed than mine?" Yes, lad, I lie ea-sy, I lie as lads would choose; I
cheer a dead man's sweet - heart,
Lento
p
Ne - ver ask me
whose.
p
p
8vb

Armida's Garden

English
Charles Hubert Hastings Parry

Respiration and Support
The rhythm of this song may be challenging for a young musician, because the time signature is variable and there is no predictable pattern for taking breaths. Nevertheless, phrases are of accessible length.

Once the singer has marked in all of the chosen breaths, he should conduct the piece. Next, conduct while mouthing the text in rhythm without sound. Consciously breathe where the breaths have been marked. Next, conduct and add spoken text in rhythm. Repeat these exercises until the breaths are secure, rhythmic and memorized.

Resonance
Dotted rhythms are found throughout this song, and the smallest note-values often have their own syllable or word, which can impede legato. To allow for consistent resonance, sing these dotted rhythms with a feeling that the shortest notes are the most vibrant, released, and free. In this exercise, elongate the vowels in notes with short rhythmic values to maintain consistent resonance.

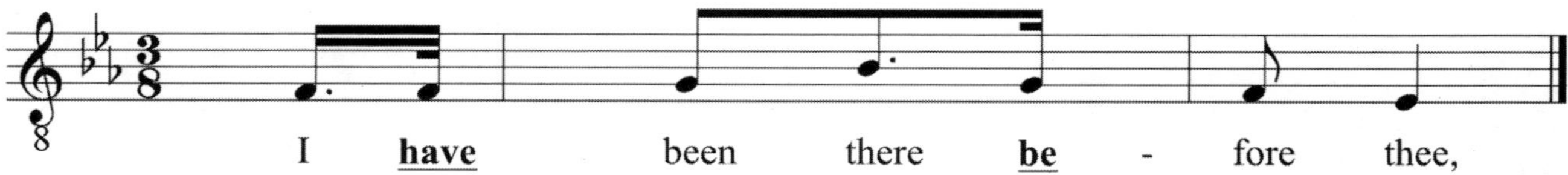

Phonation
Short notes with syllabic text setting often can lead to singing without vibrancy. Sing through this melody using [v] and [vi], being sure to maintain vibrato through the [v].

(N.B. If the singer is more visual than kinesthetic, open the piano and allow him to watch the piano strings vibrate!)

Registration

Work through the upper *passaggio* with the following exercises:

Diction/Articulation

It is especially important that the shortest note values are sung with the correct articulation. Speak through the measures with flexible articulation in rhythm at half normal speed, creating the consonants with the lips and tongue only. Gradually increase the speed to the correct tempo, keeping the same habits from the slower tempo.

Mm 4-5: I have been there before thee
Mm 9-12: Each winding way I know and all the flowers
Mm 39: When thou shalt reach it
Mm 41: God in mercy send
Mm 45: than "alas"

Phonetic Transcription of the Text

I	have	been	there	before	thee,	O	my	love!
[aːɪ	hæv	bɛn	ðɛɐ̯	bəˈfɔɐ̯	ði	o	maːɪ	lʌv]

Each	winding	way	I	know	and	all	the	flow'rs,
[it͡ʃ	ˈwaːɪn.dɪŋ	weːɪ	aːɪ	noːʊ	ænd	ɔl	ðʌ	flaːʊɐ̯z]

The	shadowy	cypress	trees,	the	twilight	grove,
[ðʌ	ˈʃæ.doːʊ.i	ˈsaːɪ.pɹɪs	tɹiz	ðʌ	ˈtwaːɪ.laːɪt	ɡɹoːʊv]

Where	rest,	in	fragrant	sleep,	the	enchanted	hours.
[ʍɛɐ̯	ɹɛst	ɪn	ˈfɹeːɪ.ɡɹənt	slip	ði	ən.ˈt͡ʃɑn.tɪd	aːʊɐ̯z]

I	have	been	there	before	thee.	At	the	end
[aːɪ	hæv	bɛn	ðɛɐ̯	bəˈfɔɐ̯	ði	æt	ði	ɛnd]

There	stands	a	gate	through	which	thou	too	must	pass.
[ðɛɐ̯	stændz	ʌ	ɡeːɪt	θɹu	ʍɪt͡ʃ	ðaːʊ	tu	mʊst	pɑs]

When	thou	shalt	reach	it,	God	in	mercy	send
[ʍɛn	ðaːʊ	ʃælt	ɹit͡ʃ	ɪt	ɡɔd	ɪn	ˈmɝ.si	sɛnd]

Thou	say	no	bitterer	word,	love,	than	"alas."
[ðaːʊ	seːɪ	noːʊ	ˈbɪ.tə.ɹɐ	wɝd	luʌ	ðæn	əˈlɑs]

Armida's Garden

From *English Lyrics:* Set 9, N.5

Mary Elizabeth Coleridge

Charles Hubert Hastings Parry
(1848-1918)

sleep, the en - chant - ed hours.
I have been there be - fore thee.
At the end There stands a
gate through which thou too must pass.
rit.
a tempo
rit.
mf
dim.
p
rit.
meno mosso
poco animando
p cresc.
poco animando
meno mosso
p
cresc.
allargando
cresc.

When thou   shalt reach it,   God   in mer-cy   send   Thou say no bit-te-rer
word,   love,____   than "a - las."
più lento
p ad lib.   a tempo
f
p
cresc.
dim.
p
*edit from original to resolve
piece for extraction from set

O Mädchen, mein Mädchen

Aria from *Friederike*
Franz Lehár

Respiration and Support

Fricatives present challenges for breath management. While these consonants need to be clear in German, it's advantageous to practice these phrases with the hand in front of the mouth to monitor air flow.

First speak and then sing this phrase with a tissue in front of the mouth, which makes it easy to evaluate breath flow.

Mir   ist   so   leicht, als   schwebt' ich   auf   lichten   Höh'n.
[miːɐ̯ ʔɪst   zoː   laːeçt   ʔals   ʃveːbt   ʔɪç   ʔaːof   ˈlɪç.tən   høːn]

Resonance

Consistent resonance and legato can be addressed through the use of voiced consonants.

O **M**ädche**n**, **m**ei**n M**ädche**n**, **[v] w**ie **l**ieb' ich dich!

Sing the melody of this aria on various voiced consonants, maintaining consistent resonance, vibrancy and lyricism in the voice.

Phonation

To ensure vibrancy in the notes of shorter duration (e.g. eighth-notes), learn this aria at a slower tempo than the indicated *allegretto*. Gradually increase the speed, maintaining vibrancy throughout.

Registration

Large leaps often present challenges for singers. Prepare these phrases on a raspberry (a lip trill with the tongue placed between the lips) and a spoken siren, noticing how the breath moves.

Maintain the released tongue position when transitioning from the raspberry to the spoken siren. Next, *sing* the sirens on the vowels found in these octave leaps.

Diction/Articulation

Transitioning from one vowel to another in the *passaggio* can be difficult. Diphthongs appear frequently in the *passaggio* in this piece. Use this exercise to help develop flexible articulation.

Prepare for the diphthongs [maːen] and [lɔːʏç.tət] in the *passaggio* using this exercise:

Phonetic Transcription and Translation of the Text

O   Mädchen, mein Mädchen, wie lieb' ich   dich!
[ʔo: ˈmɛ:t.çən   ma:en ˈmɛ:t.çən vi: lip   ɪç   dɪç]
Oh darling, my darling, how I love you!

Wie leuchtet dein Auge, wie liebst du mich!
[vi: ˈlɔ:ɤç.tət   da:en ˈʔa:o.gə vi: lipst du: mɪç]
How your eyes light up, how you love me!

Du   Blümlein   auf   dem   Feld, bist mein   alles   auf   der   Welt,
[du: ˈbly:m.la:en ʔa:of de:m fɛlt   bɪst ma:en ˈʔaləs ʔa:of de:ɐ̯ vɛlt]
You, little flower of the field, are my whole world,

du   allein   bist die, die mir gefällt!
[du: ʔa.ˈla:en bɪst di: di: mi:ɐ̯ gə.ˈfɛ:lt]
you alone are the one that I adore!

Mir   ist   so   leicht, als   schwebt ich auf   lichten Höh'n.
[mi:ɐ̯ ʔɪst zo: la:eçt ʔals ʃve:bt   ʔɪç ʔa:of ˈlɪç.tən hø:n]
I am weightless as I float, lifting to great heights.

Möchte   jedem   sagen: Bruder, die Welt ist schön!
[ˈmø:ç.tə je:.dəm ˈza:.gən ˈbru:.dɐ di: vɛlt ʔɪst ʃø:n]
I want to say to all: Brothers, the world is beautiful!

Die waldigen   Berge, das Tal,
[di: ˈvald.ɪ.gən ˈbɛr.gə das tal]
The wooded mountains and valleys,

der   Äther im   leuchtenden   Strahl,
[de:ɐ̯ ˈʔɛ:.tɐ ʔɪm ˈlɔ:ɤç.tən.dən   ʃtra:l]
the ether in the beaming rays,

sie   singen von dir,
[zi: zɪŋ.ən fɔn di:ɐ̯]
they sing of you,

jubeln   mit mir:
[ˈju:.bəln mɪt mi:ɐ̯]
rejoice with me:

O   Mädchen, mein Mädchen, wie lieb' ich   dich!
[ʔo: ˈmɛ:t.çən   ma:en ˈmɛ:t.çən vi: lip   ɪç   dɪç]
Oh darling, my darling, how I love you!

Wie leuchtet dein Auge, wie liebst du mich!
[vi: ˈlɔ:ɤç.tət   da:en ˈʔa:o.gə vi: lipst du: mɪç]
How your eyes light up, how you love me!

Du bist mein Leben, mein sonniger Schein,
[duː bɪst maːen ˈleːb.ən maːen ˈzɔn.ɪ.gɐ ʃaːen]
You are my life, my shining sun,

all meine Freude bist du nur allein,
[ʔal ˈmaːen.ə ˈfrɔːɣd.ə bɪst duː nuːɐ̯ ʔa.ˈlaɪn]
you alone are the source of my joy,

mit ganzem Herzen bin ich dein!
[mɪt ˈgant.səm ˈhɛrt.sən bɪn ʔɪç daːen]
I am yours with all my heart!

O Mädchen, o Mädchen, wie lieb ich dich!
[ʔoː ˈmɛːt.çən ʔoː ˈmɛːt.çən viː lip ʔɪç dɪç]
Oh darling, my darling, how I love you!

Wie leuchtet dein Auge, wie liebst du mich!
[viː ˈlɔːɣç.tət daːen ˈʔaːo.gə viː lipst duː mɪç]
How your eyes light up, how you love me!

Du Blümlein auf dem Feld, bist mein alles auf der Welt,
[duː ˈblyːm.laːen ʔaːof deːm fɛlt bɪst maːen ˈʔa.ləs ʔaːof deːɐ̯ vɛlt]
You, little flower of the field, are my whole world,

O Mädchen, mein Mädchen, wie lieb' ich dich!
[ʔoː ˈmɛːt.çən maːen ˈmɛːt.çən viː lip ʔɪç dɪç]
Oh darling, my darling, how I love you!

O Mädchen, mein Mädchen

from *Friederike*

Ludwig Herzer and
Fritz Löhner

Franz Lehár
(1870-1948)

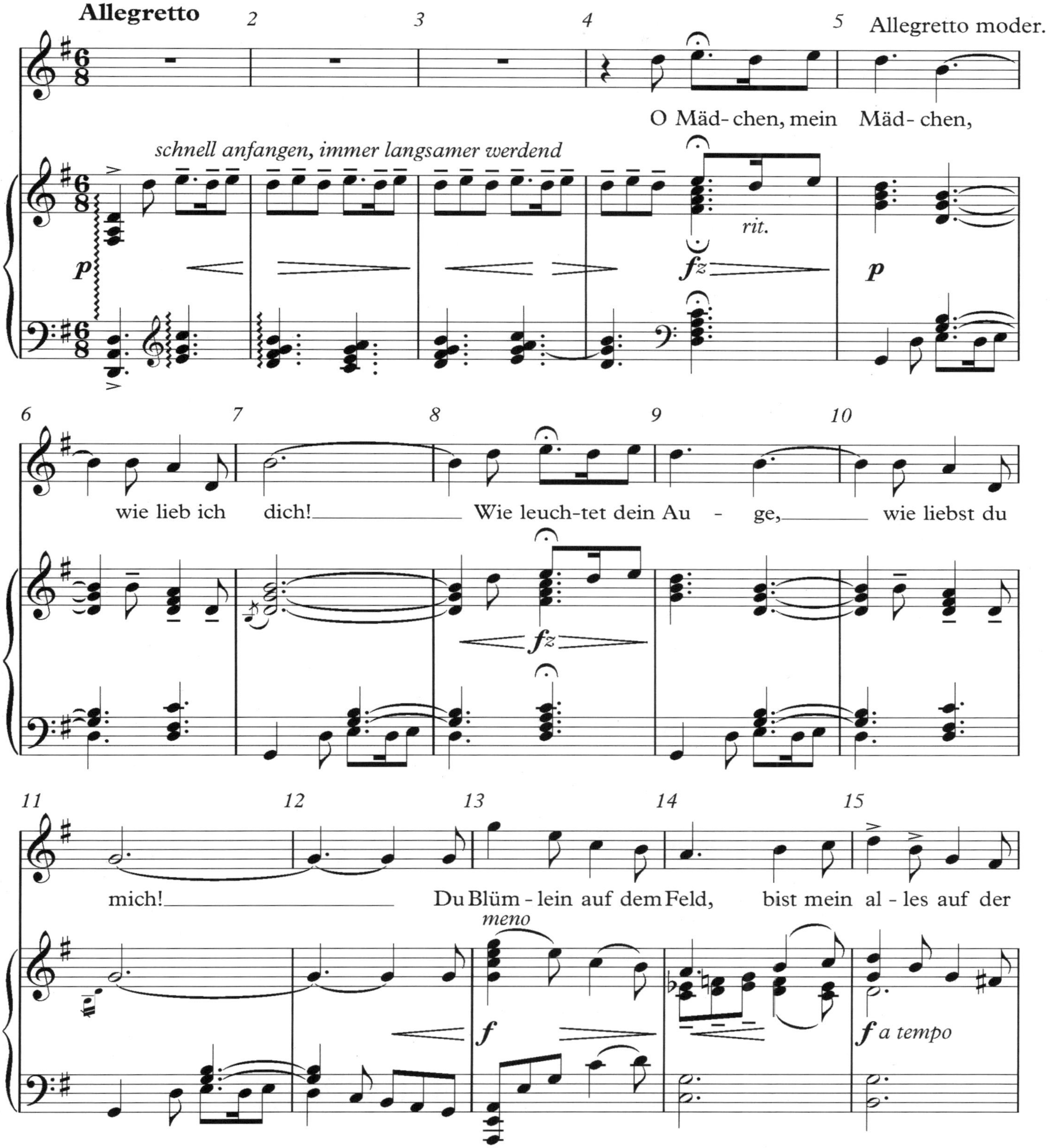

Welt, du al-lein bist die, die mir ge- fällt! Mir
bewegter
ist so leicht, als schwebt' ich auf lich-ten Höh'n. Möcht'
je - dem sa - gen: Bru - der, die Welt ist schön! Die
66

wal - di-gen Ber-ge, das Tal,_____ der Ä - ther im leuch-ten-den Strahl,
f a tempo
p
pp
sie sin-gen von dir, ju-beln mit mir._____ O Mäd-chen, mein
meno
zurückhalten
mf
fz
f
rit.
Allegretto moderato
Mäd - chen,_____ wie lieb' ich dich!_____ Wie leuch-tet dein Au - ge,_____
f a tempo
fz

wie liebst du mich!
Du bist mein Le- ben, mein son-ni-ger
Schein, all mei-ne Freu-de bist du nur al- lein,
mit gan -zem Her - zen bin ich
dein!
O Mäd-chen, mein Mäd - chen,
wie lieb' ich dich!
animato
p
cresc.
meno
f
Sehr langsam
pp
zurückhalten
rit.
p
pp fz
pp
a tempo

Wie leuch-tet dein Au - ge, wie liebst du mich! Du
Meno
Blüm - lein auf dem Feld, bist mein al - les auf der Welt! O Mäd-chen, mein
Moderato
Mäd - chen, wie lieb' ich dich!

Meiner Liebsten schöne Wangen

Aria from *Bastien und Bastienne*
Wolfgang Amadeus Mozart

Respiration and Support

Practice four measures of three beats each on a hiss, using the three/four meter of this piece in the rhythm of the melody. The body should feel active and engaged. First, rhythmically hiss the exercise below, and then intone it using the same breath flow and energy.

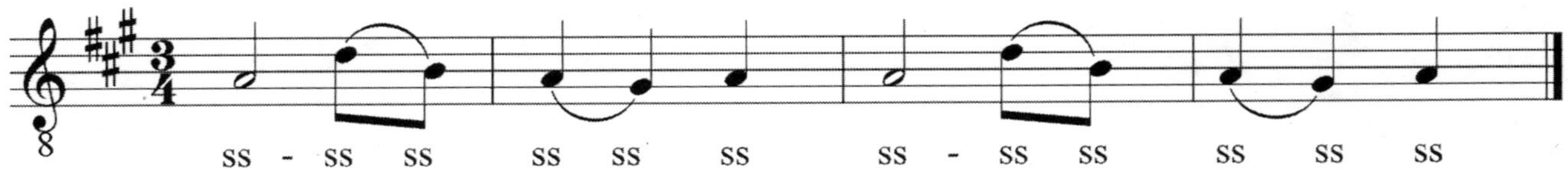

Resonance

Consider this sequence of events for creating consistent resonance in this syllabic setting. All of the systems of the voice affect resonance. Evaluate the ability of the singer to master each of these:

Posture and Alignment: tall posture, comfortably expanded chest and noble stance
Respiration and Support: buoyant ribcage and flexible abdominal muscles
Phonation: healthy onsets and offsets, consistent vibrancy
Registration: evenness in the voice from bottom to top
Articulation: relax all articulators: jaw, tongue, lips
Resonance: optimizing vocal quality, *chiaroscuro*

Resonance is the result of the former components functioning efficiently.

Phonation

To balance onset and offset in this piece, insert breaths halfway through the long phrases. This provides a better opportunity to release the last note and prepare for the following note. Be sure that each quick breath is of good quality.

Registration

To maintain an even scale in the voice, practice this vocalise, derived from measure 42, to prepare for the leap in measures 44-46.

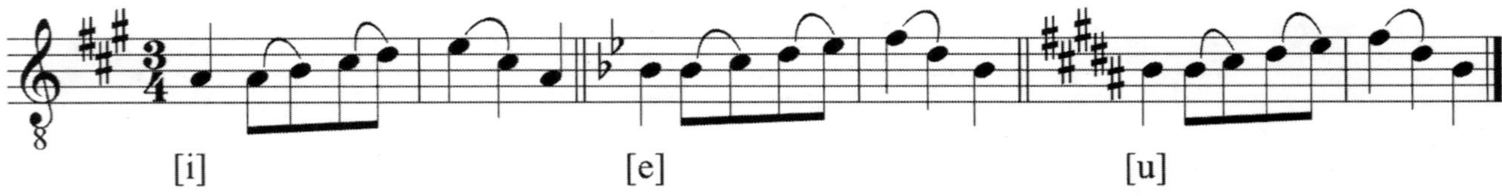

Diction/Articulation
This syllabic text setting presents challenges in articulation. In measure 13, for example, a tongue twister is found.

Speak each line slowly with legato, remembering that the vowel takes precedence.

will ich froh aufs neue sehn
bloss das Selt'ne sonst entzückt

Phonetic Transcription and Translation of the Text

Meiner   Liebsten   schöne   Wangen
[ˈmaːe.nɐ   ˈliːps.tən   ˈʃøː.nə   ˈva.ŋen]
My beloved's beautiful cheeks

will   ich   froh   aufs   neue   sehn;
[vɪl   ʔɪç   froː   ʔaːofs   ˈnɔːɣ.ə   zeːn]
I would gladly see again;

bloss   ihr   Reiz   stillt   mein   Verlangen,
[bloːs   ʔiːɐ̯   ˈraːets   ʃtɪlt   maːen   fɛɐ̯.ˈlaː.ŋen]
just her charm quiets my desire,

gold   kann   ich   um   sie   verschmäh'n.
[gɔlt   kan   ʔɪç   ʔum   ziː   fɛɐ̯.ˈʃmɛːn]
for her I can reject wealth.

Weg   mit   Hoheit,   weg   mit   Schätzen!
[vɛk   mɪt   ˈhoː.haːet   vɛk   mɪt   ˈʃɛ.tsən]
Away with royalty, away with treasures!

Eure   Pracht   wirkt   nicht   bei   mir.
[ˈʔɔːɣ.rə   praχt   vɪrkt   nɪçt   baːe   miːɐ̯]
Your splendor has no effect on me,

Nur   ein   Mädchen   kann   ergötzen
[nuːɐ̯   ʔaːen   ˈmɛːt.çən   kan   ʔɛɐ̯.ˈgœ.tsən]
A maiden can delight

hundertmal   noch   mehr   als   ihr.
[ˈhʊn.dɐ.maːl   nɔχ   meːɐ̯   ʔals   ʔiːɐ̯]
a hundred times more than they.

Wuch'rer, die   bei   stolzen   Trieben
[ˈvʊχ.rɐ   diː   baːe   ˈʃtɔl.tsən   ˈtriː.bən]
Those who wish to profit from others, who through their high taste

bloss   das   Selt'ne   sonst   entzückt,
[bloːs   das   ˈzɛlt.nə   zɔnst   ʔɛnt.ˈtsʏkt]
are only charmed by the rare

würden   ihre   Unschuld   lieben,
[ˈvʏr.dən   ˈʔiː.rə   ˈʔʊn.ʃʊlt   ˈliː.bən]
would love her innocence,

schätzen   sich   durch   sie   beglückt.
[ˈʃɛ.tsən   zɪç   dʊrç   ziː   bə.ˈglʏkt]
would consider themselves made happy through her.

Doch   umsonst,   hier   sind   die   Grenzen,
[dɔχ   ʔʊm.ˈzɔnst   hiːɐ̯   zɪnt   diː   ˈgrɛn.tsən]
But such thought is in vain, here are the limits,

sie   ist   nur   für   mich   gemacht,
[ziː   ʔɪst   nuːɐ̯   fyːɐ̯   mɪç   gə.ˈmaχt]
she was made for me alone,

und   mit   kalten   Reverenzen
[ʔʊnt   mɪt   ˈkal.tən   re.ve.ˈrɛn.tsən]
and with cold curtsies

wird   der   Reichtum   hier   verlacht.
[vɪrt   deːɐ̯   ˈraːeç.tuːm   hiːɐ̯   fɛɐ̯.ˈlaχt]
will wealth be mocked

Meiner Liebsten schöne Wangen

from *Bastien und Bastienne*

F. W. Weiskern,
J. H. F. Müller,
and J. A. Schachtner

W.A. Mozart
(1756-1791)

Tempo di Minuetto ♩ = 120

sie ver-schmäh'n, um sie ver-schmäh'n.
sie be-glückt, durch sie be-glückt.
Weg mit
Doch um-
piu f
mf
21 22 23 24 25 26 27

Ho-heit weg mit Schä-tzen! eu-re Pracht wirkt nicht bei mir;
—sonst, hier sind die Gren-zen, sie ist nur für mich ge-macht,
28 29 30 31 32 33 34

nur mein Mäd-chen kann er-gö-tzen hun-dert-mal noch mehr als
und mit kal-ten Re-ve-ren-zen, wird der Reich-tum hier ver-
mp
35 36 37 38 39 40 41

ihr, hun - dert - mal_ noch mehr als ihr, hun-dert- mal_ noch mehr_ als_
lacht, wird der_ Reich-tum hier_ ver - lacht, wird der Reich - tum hier__ ver-

ihr.
lacht.
f

Dal

Sample Rubric for Grading Repertoire

Scale of 1-5
0-20 points easy, 20-40 points moderate, 40-60 points difficult

Technical Issue Addressed	Problem Solving Questions	Scale 1-5
ACCOMPANIMENT	Is the accompaniment utilitarian, supportive, independent, etc.? Is the accompaniment part of the story line? Descriptive e.g. water figures, spinning wheel, etc.?	
CHARACTERIZATION/ACTING	Is the character appropriate to the student's dramatic capacity or life experiences? Will the student benefit from portraying this type of character?	
DICTION/ARTICULATION	Consideration of challenging consonant clusters. Closed position or difficult consonants on challenging pitches? Student's knowledge of French, Italian, Russian, German, etc. language or diction?	
DYNAMICS	Is the singer expected to sing a pianissimo high note? Are the markings pedagogically helpful (e.g. crescendo on sustained notes to assist in breath energy and/or vibrancy?)	
MELISMATIC PHRASES	Beginner or advanced melismas/melismatic phrases present? Appoggiatura? Dotted rhythms?	
MUSICAL CONSIDERATIONS	Through composed? Strophic? Accessible harmonic language? Tonal? An enjoyable melody?	
RANGE/TESSITURA	How are high notes approached—dramatically? Is the range too vast? Is the tessitura too low or high? Can a young singer sit in that particular part of the voice for that long without fatiguing?	
REGISTRATION	Does the piece assist in working through *passaggio* issues? Will the student carry weight up? Helpful vowels in an underdeveloped part of the student's voice? Etc.	
RESPIRATION	Are phrase lengths accessible? Will the breaths allow for renewal of positioning?	
TEXT SETTING	Syllabic, Patter Song, Lyric? Does the text setting assist in memorization?	
VOWELS/VOWEL SEQUENCES	Observation of vowels in *passaggio*. Will vowel patterns assist in correcting vocal faults forward to back, tongue position, etc.?	
WORDS: POETRY/LYRICS/LIBRETTO	Is this accessible poetry? Is the story age appropriate? Will the text make the memorization process difficult?	